DID YOU KNOW?
Kiwi

DID YOU KNOW?
Kiwi
young reed

Contents

What is a Kiwi? 6

Facts and figures 8

Special adaptations 10

Where do they live? 12

Feeding and breeding 14

Relatives and lookalikes 16

Kiwi in culture 18

Threats to Kiwi 20

Conserving Kiwi 22

What is a Kiwi?

- Kiwi are unique flightless **birds** that are **endemic** to **New Zealand**, meaning they are found nowhere else in the world.

- Like other birds they have **feathers** and a **beak** and **lay eggs** in a nest from which their young hatch.

- Instead of flying, Kiwi **walk around** on the **forest floor**. As New Zealand has no native land mammals these birds evolved to fill that niche, and with their fur-like plumage they even look rather mammal-like in appearance!

Brown Kiwi.

Little Spotted Kiwi.

Facts and figures

- Kiwi are about **forty to fifty centimetres long** from the tip of the beak to the tip of the tail. They usually weigh about **two or three kilograms**.
- There are **five different species** of Kiwi alive today – Little Spotted Kiwi, Great Spotted Kiwi, Southern Brown Kiwi, Okarito Brown Kiwi and North Island Brown Kiwi.
- **Māori names** for these birds include Tokoeka, Rowi, Kiwi-nui and Kiwi pukupuku.
- Their scientific name *Apteryx* comes from Ancient Greek and means **'without wings'**, although the birds do have small rudimentary wings.
- These birds can live for **fifty** or even **sixty years**.

Special adaptations

- Kiwi are the only birds in the world to have **nostrils at the end of their beak**, helping them to find food as they snuffle around on the forest floor.

- Their **strong legs and feet** help them to scrape back soil and leaf litter to get at a meal, and also dig an underground burrow for a nest.

- With no native mammal predators on New Zealand, as Kiwi evolved they **lost the power of flight**, but their **shaggy feathers** still keep the birds **warm and insulated**.

Where do they live?

- Kiwi live only on the islands that make up **New Zealand** – they are found nowhere else in the world.

- The birds used to be more widespread across New Zealand, but today they are **locally extinct** in many areas due to the presence of predators introduced by humans.

- Thankfully Kiwi can still be found in some places, where they find a home in wilder areas of **native forest**.

A young Kiwi is like a miniature version of the adult.

Kiwi egg.

Feeding and breeding

● Kiwi are **nocturnal**, meaning that they are **active at night**. They scrape the leaf litter with their **strong feet** and probe the ground for food with their **long bill**.

● The birds are mainly **insectivores**, feeding on insects, grubs and worms, although they will sometimes also eat other items such as fruit and small reptiles and amphibians.

● Kiwi **eggs are huge** for the size of the bird – up to **one fifth** of the female's body weight. They take **eighty days** of **incubation** before they hatch.

Kiwi nostrils are on the end of the long bill.

● Newly-hatched Kiwi are **precocial**. They look like mini versions of the adults and don't need help from their parents – they can **fend for themselves** straight away.

Relatives and lookalikes

- Kiwi are part of the **Ratite** family of birds, which includes other flightless species such as **Ostrich** and **Emu**.
- New Zealand was once home to another family of Ratites, the **Moas** that could grow to **three metres** tall, although Kiwi are considered to be more closely related to the **Cassowaries** of Australia and New Guinea.
- Kiwi are often confused with **Weka**, which are similar in shape and colour and are also flightless. However, Weka belong to the **Rail family** and are not closely related to Kiwi.
- These rails are much more confiding than Kiwi, so if the bird you're looking at is trying to **steal your sandwiches** from your backpack it'll be a **Weka**!

Cassowary.

Weka.

Statue of the now-extinct Moa.

Kiwi in culture

- Humans seem to hold Kiwi in awe, perhaps due to their unique appearance and nature. The birds have long been of **cultural significance to Māori people.**

- Since Europeans arrived in New Zealand, Kiwi have been adopted as a **symbol for the modern nation.** Perhaps reflecting the charisma and endearing qualities of the birds, the New Zealand people have come to be known as **'Kiwis'.**

- Kiwi feature commonly as the subject for statues, sculptures and other **artworks**, and on the likes of **currency** and **postage stamps**, logos for **sports teams** and **businesses**, and even on **coats of arms**.
- A fruit has famously adopted the Kiwi name, perhaps because the **kiwi fruit** has a rounded shape and rough brown skin that bears something of a resemblance to its namesake bird?

Feral dog.

Threats to Kiwi

- In total, including members of all five species, there are thought to be less than **seventy thousand** Kiwi alive today.
- Some species are classified as **Endangered** or **Vulnerable** by the New Zealand government.
- The main threats to their survival include **losing their forest habitat** due to **human activities** such as agriculture and industry.
- Some Kiwi are killed by **road-traffic accidents** .

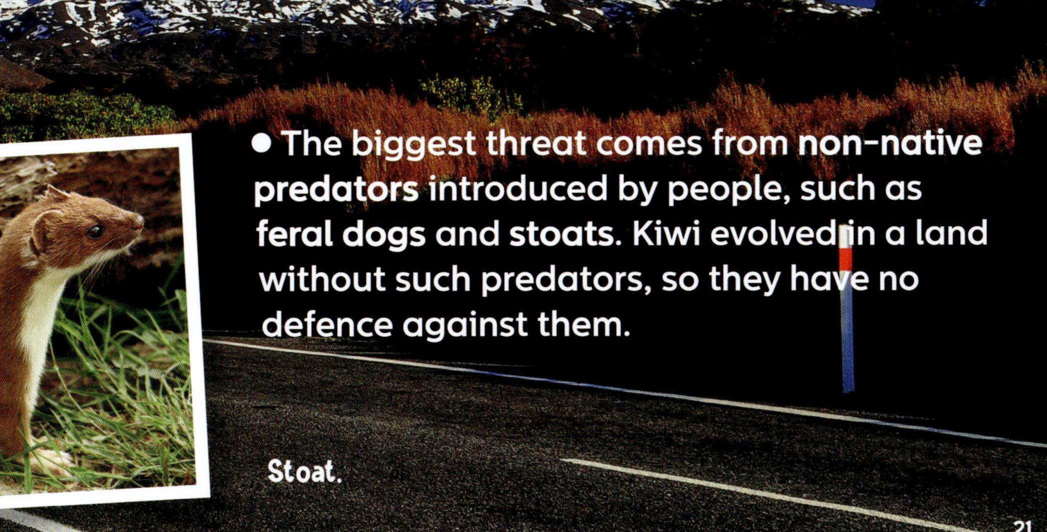

- The biggest threat comes from **non-native predators** introduced by people, such as **feral dogs and stoats.** Kiwi evolved in a land without such predators, so they have no defence against them.

Stoat.

Conserving Kiwi

- To help save Kiwi from **extinction**, some birds have been moved to **predator-free sanctuaries** and **islands**, where they have a better chance of surviving and raising young.
- Kiwi are also **bred in captivity** and then once they are old enough they can be **released into the wild**, often into sanctuaries such as the ones mentioned above.
- It is vitally important to **tell people about Kiwi**, so that they know to protect their habitat and the birds themselves, for example by not taking pet dogs into Kiwi territory.

Predator-free island sanctuaries such as Tiritiri Matangi near Auckland (main image) have been a success for conserving Kiwi.

First published in 2025 by
New Holland Publishers

newhollandpublishers.com

A record of this book is held at the National Library of Australia.

ISBN 9781760798079

OTHER TITLES IN THE 'DID YOU KNOW?' SERIES:

Capybara
ISBN 9781760798048

Dolphins
ISBN 9781921078000

Kangaroos
ISBN 9781921073861

Kea
ISBN 9781760798062

Koala
ISBN 9781921073878

Lizards
ISBN 9781921073885

Meerkat
ISBN 9781921073892

Penguins
ISBN 9781921073908

Red Panda
ISBN 9781921073915

Sharks
ISBN 9781921078017

Tasmanian Devil
ISBN 9781760798055

For details of these books and hundreds of other Natural History titles see newhollandpublishers.com